The Shape of a Girl

Jewel

The Shape of a Girl

Jewel

Joan MacLeod

Talonbooks
2002

Talonbooks
P.O. Box 2076
Vancouver, BC, V6B 3S3, Canada
www.talonbooks.com

Typeset in Scala and printed and bound in Canada.

Seventh Printing: October 2008

The publisher gratefully acknowledges the financial support of the Canada Council for the Arts; the Government of Canada through the Book Publishing Industry Development Program; and the Province of British Columbia through the British Columbia Arts Council for our publishing activities.

Rights to produce *The Shape of a Girl* or *Jewel* in whole or in part, in any medium by any group, amateur or professional, are retained by the author. Interested persons are requested to apply to her agent: Catherine Knights, 3SG Talent Management, 45 Charles Street East, LL7, Toronto, Ontario, Canada M4Y 1S2; Tel: (416) 925-9009; Fax: (416) 925-7557; Email: cknights@canadafilm.com.

National Library of Canada Cataloguing in Publication Data

MacLeod, Joan, 1954-
   The shape of a girl ; Jewel

   Plays.
   ISBN 978-0-88922-460-5

   I. Title. II. Title: Jewel.
PS8575.L4645S52 2002   C812'.54   C2002-910068-2
PR9199.3.M33429S52 2002

Contents

Introduction

Joan MacLeod's plays celebrate the creative, empathetic imagination. In *Toronto, Mississippi* a young woman ignores the banality of geographical fact in favour of her own imaginative truth. In each of the other major plays—*Jewel, The Hope Slide, Amigo's Blue Guitar, 2000* and *The Shape of a Girl*—a female character reaches across time and space, imagining herself into other people's experiences of atrocity or disaster in a dramatic universe verging on the apocalyptic. The empathetic protagonist hears of people buried by falling mountains, swallowed by giant seas, tortured by their schoolmates or countrymen. She vividly reconstructs the terror and loss, then tries to make sense of the experience and the lives affected by it, including her own. In MacLeod's plays the self is ineluctably connected to the world. The personal and political intertwine. Hope slides but despair is kept at bay.

Framing the first sixteen years of Joan MacLeod's playwriting career, *Jewel* (1985) and *The Shape of a Girl* (2001) have a great deal in common. Both are monologues grounded in historically specific Canadian tragedies: the 1982 sinking of the oil rig *Ocean Ranger* off the coast of Newfoundland, and the 1997 killing of Victoria schoolgirl Reena Virk. In both monologues fictional female characters bear witness, though neither has been at the site of the tragedy. Theirs is an imaginative witness, an empathetic reconsideration of the experience. Both address an absent male auditor. In each case the character imagines herself momentarily possessing divine power. "You'd think I was God or something," Braidie observes in *The Shape of a Girl*. *Jewel*'s Marjorie pictures herself reaching down "like the hand of God" to save a man from drowning in the towering waves of the frigid North Atlantic. But neither play finally allows for anything more than the necessities and possibilities of the strictly human.

Jewel is a spoken Valentine's greeting addressed by Marjorie to her late husband, Harry, on the third anniversary of his death in the *Ocean Ranger* disaster. They had been married for just a few years when Harry left their home on the border between northern B.C. and Alberta to take a lucrative short-term job in the booming offshore oil fields four thousand miles away. Living alone in their trailer, Marjorie grieves aloud, reminiscing about other Valentine's days and her courtship with Harry. She recalls how she received the news of the sinking, how she processed his death. These are the play's most powerful passages. Marjorie's empathetic imagination brings the past alive in the immediate present, taking concrete form in MacLeod's gift for descriptive language and in the physical presence of the solitary actor. As she recounts the stages of her grief—anger and disbelief, regret, blame, and guilt (that of the rig's corporate owners as well as her own)—we realize that Marjorie is not entirely alone. She has access to family support systems, a grieving workshop, a widows' group. She also has her good friend Deb and a new relationship with a man. But she can only fully re-experience Harry's death and its aftermath alone in his presence. We get the sense that she has communed with Harry in spirit before. But this time the retelling and reliving will be cathartic. For Marjorie (though MacLeod would never use such a cliché), this is the first day of the rest of her life.

For Braidie it is the first week. Like Marjorie, she feels compelled to speak. For both women, silence and the status quo have become intolerable. A theatrical monologue, like any other fictive first-person narrative, is a confession, an explanation, a plea for understanding or forgiveness. Its immediate motivation is usually some particular event that has brought matters to a crisis. Marjorie the night before has crossed a line. Braidie the week before has broken a taboo. Doing so causes a major readjustment of their most important relationships. Funny and bratty and smart, teenage Braidie chooses to confess and explain to her older brother, Trevor, who has moved away to Whistler. Unlike

Marjorie, Braidie gets no help from her parents. In fact "the voice of mum" is one of her and Trevor's running jokes. She can't confide in her girlfriends because they are directly involved and, anyway, now they shun her. Trevor has been heroic before and would likely be sympathetic. So why doesn't Braidie phone him or even go tell him in person? Maybe it would just be too hard, too shameful for her actually to admit some of the things she has done or failed to do. She needs to accuse, understand, and forgive herself. Absent, Trevor is her ideal audience.

Braidie spends the whole play on an island (probably Bowen Island, near Vancouver) across the bay from a camp for blind children. Her isolation and blindness co-exist in tension with the connectedness and insight her acute imaginative intelligence affords her. It's no accident that she wants to be a poet like Stevie Smith or Adrienne Rich, from whose lines the play's title is taken. Like Marjorie, Braidie slides back and forth in time, layering the events of the present with scenes of her life before the fall. We watch the superficial innocence of her girlhood move inexorably towards adult horrors and responsibilities that can no longer be denied. She becomes obsessed with the Reena Virk story (never mentioned by name but unmistakable in its details), especially the girl's tormentors, even before consciously admitting to herself her own involvement in something potentially similar. She senses that she could be, that maybe she already is, one of them: a monster in the shape of a girl. But imaginative identification is only a catalyst. In the face of her friend Sofie's torment, Braidie finally has to act. She does the unthinkable when doing nothing becomes unbearable. "That's the trouble with staying silent," Braidie says. "I can't move, even when I want to." In both these plays speech is a powerful commitment to action. Speaking aloud gives concrete form to what imagination has conjured and intuited, activating the intelligence to digest implications and determine consequences. The stakes are somewhat higher in Braidie's case than in Marjorie's, though each in her own way deals with issues of life and death. Giving voice to what she feels and knows allows Braidie to move herself and others to act, and Marjorie to take hold of her life and move on.

—Jerry Wasserman

for Urjo,
for everything

The Shape of a Girl

Acknowledgements

This play was written with the generous support of The Canada Council, The B.C. Arts Council and The Banff Centre. Thanks also to the good folk at both Green Thumb and A.T.P. and to Ann (Annie) Silberman, Liz Hines, Leslie Jones and Mariette MacLeod. Thank you to Brian Pincott, Scott Reid, Ian Tamblyn and especially Patrick McDonald and the brave and remarkable Jenny Young—what a team. And finally, thank you to my husband Bill and my daughter Ana—both gave a lot so that this play could be written.

The Shape of a Girl was commissioned by Green Thumb Theatre and was first produced at Alberta Theatre Projects, a co-production with Green Thumb, as part of the PanCanadian Playrites Festival in February 2001 in Calgary with the following cast:

BRAIDIE   Jenny Young

Director: Patrick McDonald
Costume Designer: David Boechler
Lighting Designer: Brian Pincott
Set & Properties Designer: Scott Reid
Composer: Ian Tamblyn
Production Stage Manager: Dianne Goodman
Stage Manager: Rhonda Kambeitz
Assistant Stage Manager: Rikki Schlosser
Junior Apprentice: Janna Brunnen

In the fall of 2001 Green Thumb remounted the original production of *The Shape Of A Girl* for a national tour.

The Shape of a Girl is a one act, one character play. Braidie is a fifteen-year-old female. The running time is approximately eighty minutes; there is no intermission.

The original set was a gravel beach with a large and beautiful driftwood tree upstage.

Darkness, a bell sounds from the distance, spot up on BRAIDIE, *she speaks to her absent brother Trevor.*

BRAIDIE

I woke up this morning to this sound. This sound that feels far away one second then from right inside my gut the next. Very pure with the potential to be extremely creepy. But before I've even opened my eyes this other thing worms its way in and wreaks its usual havoc: the voice of mum.

I tell you Trevor, she's gotten even worse since you left. She is yelling that THIS *is* IT. What IT is I still haven't figured out. At this point in my life being kicked out would be incredible. All I know is her voice chiseled, no burrowed into my brain before I was fully conscious. By the time I'm actually awake the voice of mum has reached this pitch that is making the panelling beside my bed vibrate. *Braidie—I have had* IT!

And then I remembered that day, that truly outstanding day Trevor when you told mum that in another life her voice is going to come back as an ear wig. I was thinking of that exact thing when that sound comes again and this time I know what it is. The blind are back, back at their summer camp across the bay—which is highly weird because it's hardly April. That sound is the gong that tells the blind folks to get up or come for porridge. It just seems like it's really close, sound carrying across water and all that.

And for some reason today, on this particular morning, at this particular point in time, after living on this stupid island my whole life, I am acutely aware for the first time that sound carries across water BOTH ways. Did that ever dawn on you? Did you ever have this really ugly image of mum's voice snaking around the blind camp? There they are: lying on their bunk beds, innocent as pie. *You're your own worst enemy!* That'll get them sitting up or worse yet shuffling off to the cook shack, mum's voice attacking them from above like some crow gone nuts. *Keep your shoulders back! You are walking like an ape!*

I am thinking of all these things Trevor and how I wish I could talk to you about it. I wish you were here, asleep in your room. You, big brother, with the unparalleled ability to sleep

until three in the afternoon three months in a
row; you who can drive all the way to your
place in Whistler using only your peripheral
vision. I am thinking of all this stuff then all of
a sudden this seaplane lands, right outside the
deck. I pretend, just like we always did, that the
plane is here to kill us. BAM! BAM! BAM!—it'll
dive-bomb the whole island. Bullets will
explode the mattress around me, outline my
arms, my legs.

That is how my day begins, that is how I
greet the morning. And from across the water
the gong from the camp sounds again. I think,
briefly, very briefly, about actually going to
school. I also contemplate apologizing to mum
for the basic snarkiness of my disposition—all
inherited of course—but she's already left for
work. Then I'm pretending we're all Muslims
or Buddhist monks or anything except who we
are. And that the gong is calling us to prayer or
at least ending this round.

That the sound means—STOP, don't move a
muscle, help is on the way.

*

I watch the school bus come and go. I haven't
been to school in a week now. Adrienne always
waits until the last minute to climb aboard. She
looks tall and grumpy. Mum says I need to

make more friends. She reminds me that in grade five I almost had a heart attack because Adrienne and I had different teachers for the first time, the first time since pre-school. In preschool Annie made a point of trying to let other kids sit beside Adrienne at circle and I'd just freak. And Annie and me, we'd have to go off together for a quiet time in her rocking chair. She smelled like play dough. I'd bury my head in her shirt and I'd blubber all over Annie. The world was ending. I love Adrienne so much I used to worry I was a lesbian and when dad would say stuff like *you two sure are joined at the hip!* I thought he was worried that I was a lesbian too.

If Adrienne jumped off the Lions Gate Bridge would you? All over the world, parents have been posing this question to their children forever. I used to think I'd want to be dead if mum or dad died. Now I actually imagine them dead so that I'll be able to stay out late and do what I want. If Adrienne jumped off the Lions Gate I wouldn't follow BUT—I would spend the rest of my life writing poems about her short one. And explaining the devastating effect that her death had on, well, her obviously. And me. I'm not the suicidal type. Even if I was a complete mess and my brain had turned to jello I wouldn't want anyone pulling the plug.

Mum would pull the plug on me in a second. Remember that Trevor. Make sure mum doesn't pull the plug.

So the bus is gone and mum is gone and even though it is my intention to at least try and write a poem I end up flipping on the TV. I watch one of those really bad shows about really bad things that happen to really depressingly normal people. We're still not allowed cable so the reception is just rancid—everybody's foreheads have gone alien and bodies all shivery—like when you'd try to zap down something racy from Pay. The show's called MOST DANGEROUS AND AWFUL MOMENTS EVER.

They're showing this speedboat, this speedboat in Florida somewhere and it's heading full speed, dead ahead, for this big bleacher full of spectators. God knows what the problem with the boat is but the guy driving it is yelling and waving his hands, warning the people in the stands to get the hell out of the way. The boat smashes right into the crowd—chaos. I tell you—blood and guts and totally nuts.

And I was thinking of this poet, this poet I have recently discovered called Stevie Smith. Not a guy Stevie, a girl Stevie. I was thinking of this thing she said that I loved, that reminded me of my friends and me This thing about not waving but drowning. I was thinking of that when the rabbit ears sort of shake, almost like they're one of those divining things and all of a sudden the whole scene changes on the TV.

And there we are. A group of girls—just like me and Adrienne and Jackie and Amber. A group of girls with hair and jeans and jackets. *They are not waving, they are drowning.* And this group of girls on the TV starts waving, right on cue. Weird I'm thinking. This is highly weird.

And what feels even stranger is that the picture is actually clear for once, from the neck down at least. But their faces are blurry, smudged, almost as though someone has taken an eraser and tried to rub them out.

And then I realize who these girls are. They are supposed to look distorted because they are young offenders and we aren't allowed to see who they are. They are accused of assault, accused of murder, accused of killing another girl—a fourteen-year-old girl. One is wearing these big high heel runners like Amber's. They are all standing out front of the courthouse while the judge is taking a break. They are laughing like maniacs. Me and Adrienne often laugh like maniacs. Honestly, totally unprovoked.

Then the news guy starts talking about how one saw her dad murdered when she was six. And another girl's dad was also murdered. And

I feel stupid to have ever thought we have anything in common. In fact it pisses me off that they are trying to pass themselves off as normal. And even though it's illegal to do so, I can imagine their faces: slutty eyes, chapped lips. Then one girl waves again and yells *hi* and you just know she's making goofy faces just like Adrienne and me did when we saw the Canucks, when we thought we were making our debut on national television.

I don't know why I have to find out more about those girls, I just do. They are all over the news. Always in a group, always from the back or with their jackets pulled over their heads. I don't want to look at the victim, it's too depressing. But she is everywhere too—as a baby with her dad, as a regular weird kid on holiday, then one of those blown up yearbook pictures that always mean someone is either a movie star or dead.

And then that gong across the bay starts ringing again. Except this time it sounds like a summons, like someone is calling me.

Lights up on set—BRAIDIE is on a beach, perhaps leaning against a log, looking out at the water, she is wearing jeans, a warm jacket, a tangle of blackberry vines and bush rise up steeply on the bank behind.

27

Hello! I'm here ... Attention: Braidie has landed.

Braidie looks upstage.

But up at the camp the shutters are all still up, the flag pole is bare, not a blind guy in sight. And you know that gong? It's just the same old bell. I was expecting something out of Tarzan. So it's me, solo. Braidie on the beach. Remember how much we used to love coming here to spy?

Braidie holds her arms, straight out in front.

Trevor, let's be blind.

Shutting her eyes.

Shut your eyes and you can hear the summer. The little kids arriving, so wired up. And the older ones with their dogs, those outstanding dogs. I love Buster but I've always felt he was an inferior species of animal. I mean I've never seen a seeing-eye dog eating goose shit or sniffing up another retriever.

A bell rings softly in the distance, Braidie opens her eyes and looks up the bank, watching a memory from years ago.

Trevor? Did you hear that? Do you see? It's Sofie, twelve years old. The camp is deserted like now. It's winter. I am below her, also twelve. Adrienne is up the hill beside Sofie,

always nearly one year older. Sofie wants to
ring the bell because she thinks Adrienne
might kill her and I think Adrienne might kill
Sofie too. I watch Adrienne watching Sofie.
Adrienne is so mad her mouth is shaking.
Sofie is watching me. She has no idea my body
has turned to concrete. I can't move and I can't
shout. All I can do is see.

*

*BRAIDIE goes back in time, she is eight years old,
she gallops around and around until she falls
over, exhausted and happy.*

We are in love, we are all forever in love. We
spend hours drawing them. We call ourselves
by our new names in secret: Rainbow Rider,
Lucky Lady, Thunder. We cram our pockets and
lunchkits with them—piles and piles of ponies.
Little brushes for their tiny pink manes, their
purple tails.

Sofie is the new girl in grade two. Her horse
name is Trotter and Toto and Lala and Gypsy.
Because Sofie doesn't just fall in love with
horses and have a horse name like the rest of
us. Sofie becomes a horse or sometimes an
entire herd of horses. She gallops out to the
playground for recess; she trots down the halls.
She talks by doing whinnies and stomping her

feet. She even eats her lunch like it's a feed-bag, without using her hands.

We are amazed by Sofie, how she can spend hours, entire afternoons, down there on all fours. How she never cares about who sees. *Good little horsie.* That's what Adrienne says and then Adrienne is flying, having been bucked by Sofie the horse onto the couch. And then Rachel has a turn on Sofie's back and Sofie sends her flying too. We love Sofie the horse. We make tiny braids all over her head; we paint rainbows on her cheeks.

And then one day, one normal un-special day Adrienne comes to school and announces that it's penalty day. We don't know what penalty day is. Adrienne explains that on penalty day one girl is chosen and everyone is mean to that one girl for the whole day. *Why?* Adrienne doesn't know. It's just a part of school. Adrienne offers to go first. We get to be mean to her first. I want to go first too.

At first penalty day is hard to figure out. There are a lot of rules. The person we have to be mean to has fleas of course. Everyone has to write FP for flea proof on their hand.

BRAIDIE, *as a teenager again.*

You know something Trevor? By the end of grade four penalty day had become as complex

30

as World War Two. But who the enemy was had become entirely simple. Now all the girls had FP written on their hands, all the girls but one. I don't know why it was Sofie. It just was.

*

It is the next day, BRAIDIE is settling in on the beach.

THE VOICE OF MUM came in weak today, this annoying little signal that was barely registering. I believe I told her I was sick—perhaps I surfaced long enough to tell her school was out of the question. I sense she senses that school and myself are on our last legs. Maybe I'll be like you, try homeschooling. Maybe I'll move up to Whistler too.

Mum and me did have a big blow out last night, a major blow out. She says to me, all weird and cheery—*the teen centre is having a dance this weekend. Why don't you go?* I point out I went last time and that it was BEYOND repulsive.

She points out that I never actually went inside, that I hung out with Adrienne in the parking lot. How does she know?

Because she drove by—MORE than once. She cruised the teen centre like an undercover cop or a pervert. Life with her is unbearable, a lesson in indignity.

In today's papers there are no pictures of those young offenders. I tell you—it's almost a relief. You remember when the girl was killed Trevor, you were still living here. How she was beat up by a group of girls and this guy and then finished off a few minutes later by that boy and this one girl who went back for more. The ones that watched the girl get beat up, they aren't accused of anything. To be accused you have to have gotten in there, down and dirty. I suppose that to be a teenager, even to be a little kid, is to often see very hideous behaviour from your peers.

If you reported everyone you would certainly have to watch your back at all times and look no one in the face, ever. You would have to go through your entire life using only your peripheral vision.

The girls who beat her up, the girls who are on trial for assault, they used to hang out at Walmart. They also hang out UNDER COVER. This sounds way cooler than it is. Because under cover really is just that—a covered area at the school just like we had for playing hopscotch when it rained. But these really are tough girls. They make like they are a gang and that they're all hooked up with the gangs in New York and L.A.

On Granville Mall once Adrienne and me were followed by some tough girls, these wipe out girls. They wanted us to give them some money and Adrienne said no way. They said they were going to get us. One gobbed on the back of Adrienne's jeans. But we weren't afraid of them. We just thought they were idiots.

These girls in Victoria, they're a mess. Some are in foster care, some have been doing the McFamily thing for a long long time. Some have already been up on charges, one for lighting fire to another girl's hair. The fight with the dead girl starts when someone butts out a cigarette on her forehead. This is terrible enough in itself but it also opens a door. *Look what I did? Now just watch, just wait and see ...* It's surreal. And that's not fair to say because it's exactly the opposite—it's totally real. I mean it happened. And what scares me, what freaks me right out Trevor is that I know the way in. I don't know how else to put it. I know the way in.

The human body is what? Eighty percent water? That kills me. We're like these melons with arms and legs. Well eighty percent of the female brain is pure crap. We're constantly checking each other out, deciding who goes where, who's at the bottom.

When I look at her picture, when I look at the picture of the dead girl in the paper, part of me gets it. And I hate it that I do; I hate to be even partly composed of that sort of information. But right now, if you put me in a room filled with girls, girls my age that I've never seen before in my life—I could divide them all up. I could decide who goes where and just where I fit in without anyone even opening their mouth. They could be from this island, they could be from Taiwan. It doesn't matter. Nobody would have to say a word. You know something Trevor? I could have divided up a room like that when I was in grade two. Grade fucking two.

*

When the lights come up BRAIDIE *is ten years old, being Adrienne, perhaps standing up the bank, up high.*

No one is to have contact of any kind with IT *from first period until lunch. If you have to address* IT *do so during homeroom. On the school bus* IT *has to sit on the fourth seat on the left. If* IT *talks to any boys it will be dealt with by me.* IT*'s lunch today will be divided between Amber, Braidie and Jackie. Case closed.* IT *will make no comments and will not be allowed to look at me anymore as of now.*

BRAIDIE *leaps down.*

Adrienne then turns her back on Sofie, to show us she means business. Adrienne always means business. So the five of us sit there, waiting for the school bus.

Yesterday means nothing now; it means nothing that we spent all day Sunday together and had a good time. There is a brand new code every day. I spend most of my time trying to figure out what the code is.

—*What if she...*
—IT.
—*What if* IT *has to go to the bathroom.*

This is Amber interjecting when she shouldn't. Adrienne ignores her. Adrienne often ignores what isn't important. And it works.

Yesterday we let ourselves into one of the houses Adrienne's mum is trying to sell. *Let's take off our tops.* Adrienne is lifting up her tee-shirt. She is wearing a white bra covered in tiny pink flowers. Mine is identical. Sofie yanks up her blouse. She is wearing a rolled up under-shirt.

—IT'S A SPORTS BRA, *says Sofie.*
—IT *thinks that's a bra.*
—DON'T CALL ME THAT.
—*Don't call me that.*

The house is freezing. The beds are all bare. The mattresses and the ocean silver. Something shitty's going to happen. Something shitty could happen here. *Tell* IT *to get us something from the fridge.* And Sofie does. She comes back with a box of baking soda and a jar of relish. The lousy food is Sofie's fault. Maybe she should've broken in early and stocked the fridge. I would've. I would've done that if I was in her position. But Sofie doesn't have a clue. She has no sense of how to avoid anything.

A sports bra, says Adrienne, is a defense against guys. The really high end sports bras repel guys, totally impenetrable. A good sports bra will catapult guys across the room. THAT *is* NOT *a sports bra. It's a little Miss Undie Undie shirt.*

Ha ha. Another one of Sofie's bad habits, ha-ha-ing all the time. She sticks her fingers into the jar of relish. *Ooohhhh Gross.* Adrienne practically has a heart attack. It is gross. Sofie slopping up a jar of hamburger relish. Except now Adrienne also finds it funny. And all of a sudden everyone is laughing and Sofie is allowed to be our friend again.

So we sit there all afternoon in our bras or our phony bras, fingers in the relish. Last year we took off all our clothes and sat together in a dry bathtub. I don't know why. We just did.

—You have to swim across this lake to get there.
Then you'll come to a little door in the side of a
tree.

This is Adrienne, doing what we always do.
Designing a place, a home for the four of us. A
dream house where we will all live together
forever.

My dream house always looks the same—one
big room that is divided by gauzy white
curtains, sort of like a swishy hospital ward.
There are no mothers and our dads will show
up with supplies only when we want them to.
Boys are banished. We do not want boys like
the ones we see now, getting on the school bus.
Adrienne, Sofie, Amber and me are first picked
up and last home everyday on the school bus.

BRAIDIE, *as a teenager again.*

You were there too Trevor. At the back with
the boys: throwing pencil cases and shoes and
sweaters out the window. You had a handmade
sling shot that was the envy of everyone. And a
pocketful of smooth black stones. You were
always pummeling each other, always
mouthing off to Gustaf the driver. So you
probably didn't notice how we sat around Sofie.
And how still she was, with her eyes straight
ahead. Behind her Jackie was kicking her
calves, something was smeared in her hair. The
girls across from her were chanting but you'd

37

have to listen hard to hear it. While you boys in the back were slugging it out we were in the front, almost still, always the good little girls.

*

A few days later.

The voice of mum and I went out for dinner last night. As usual Dad—also known as Planet Dad—is away on business, so it's going to be, and I quote—*just us girls.*

One would think that dinner would mean ordering food, eating food, paying for food. Not so. Mum insists, first, that we sit at the same table. Two, that I don't read. Three, four, and five that I get my hair out of my face, sit up properly and stop looking as though I'm planning my escape. And six, she wants us to *reconnect*, have ourselves a little chat. I explain, patiently, that I'd rather be shot from a cannon than hang around and see what she really has up her stupid sleeve.

And so it comes out: the school has phoned her at work. They are seeking an explanation for my unexplained absences. I explain, patiently, that I am now homeschooling.

All apparently news to mum. And news to the school.

I am part way through stating just what I think homeschooling should be when the voice of mum jumps to her feet and starts doing the famous whisper-shriek. *This is the last straw, the end of the road, the end of the rope, the absolute limit.* Then she's goes. Leaves me sitting there alone with Terry the cook. Terry leers from the kitchen. He cleans his teeth with a business card and winks at me.

The Braidie Institute Of Higher Learning. Lesson One—Current Events

BRAIDIE *holds up a newspaper.*

Girls Turning On Each Other
Bullied To Death
Girls Killing Girls

These are the headlines, these are what put us on the map. Like the Stanley Cup riots only worse, way worse.

The articles go on and on about how girls are getting meaner. The attacks more vicious. I look at those girls. I look at the pictures of those young offenders until the newspaper goes all squirrelly. If you look at them in bits they are regular girls: these lips, that hair, those kind of jeans.

If someone could invent a laser to zap the rotten parts they would be entirely normal. Young offenders. *Sorry—I didn't mean to offend you!* Adrienne and me would run into people on purpose on the ferry so that we could say that. *Oooops! No offense ...* We thought that was hysterical.

A girl in the shape of a monster
A monster in the shape of a girl

That, Trevor, is poetry. It is also a riddle that gets played out in Victoria. Because that's how they treat her—like a monster. Only they're the monsters, get it? Because they phoned her up. *Guess what we're doing? Wanna come?* It's like wolves pretending to be some animal that's hurt, maybe a little calf or a goat. This wasn't a case of someone in the wrong place at the wrong time. This was planned, organized.

And the girl, she knows they're one scary bunch but she goes. Maybe she is pleased that someone phoned, someone wanted her to do something. *Let's meet here ...* She even brings her pyjamas. Her pyjamas and diary and Charlie perfume are buckled into her black pack.

> BRAIDIE *goes back in time, she is twelve years old.*

Sofie walks like a cripple, little quarters of blood on her heel, soaking into her white socks. Sofie wears her runners too small because her feet are too big. She is accused of

40

watching the girls get undressed in gym. But I
watch too. I want to see who else has hair
under their arms or who has thighs as big as
mine. I talked to her after volley ball. I told her,
I did the best I could.

—*Sofie don't go on the field trip.* See—I said it: in
plain English.
—*Why?*
—*Just don't.*
—*But we have to write an essay.*

This is pure Sofie, putting homework ahead
of life or death. I tell you—she's an extremely
exasperating person. We are all going to see
Hamlet for the field trip, at a theatre in town.
It's not the real *Hamlet*; it's a phony version for
kids.

FOR EMERGENCY ONLY—SORTIE DU
SECOURS. I have studied that sign ever since I
can remember. It is written over top of some
windows in the bus. I sit three rows down from
Sofie. Jackie and Adrienne are behind me.

Sofie is sitting with Lorna. Lorna's dad owns
the store on our island; sometimes she works
there. We don't know Lorna. We don't even
think of Lorna as an actual person.

The ocean shrinks and glitters as we head
over the Lions Gate. You can see where we live,
lying out there in the strait, all wrapped up in

mist. It looks uninhabited, prehistoric.
Adrienne and Lorna have switched places.
Adrienne is whispering something to Sofie.
Sofie is looking dead ahead. Adrienne leans
into Sofie so that Sofie is squished up against
the side. Sofie's face turns grey.

FOR EMERGENCY ONLY. Sofie pushes the
window on the bus. It fans out unnaturally
from the bottom. Sofie hoists herself up, her
head is out. Sofie is going to jump out the
window. The ocean is hundreds of feet below.

I shut my eyes. And Sofie is falling, cannon-
balling over the side of the bridge, her clothes
parachute around her, a gigantic flower. I open
my eyes. Sofie hasn't gone over the side of
anything. Her bum is stuck in the window of
the bus.

Amber and Adrienne and me and Jackie—we
laugh so hard we nearly puke. Sofie is all weird
and breathing heavy. Then she pushes out a
sound that is hardly human. *Ha-ha.*

The bus driver is grabbing Sofie by the
sweater. He pulls her in. *What the hell do you
think you're doing?* Adrienne watches Sofie.
Nothing, Sofie says. *Fooling around.*

Sofie isn't allowed to see the play. We watch
Ophelia load herself up with flowers and sail

off to meet her maker. We make burp noises except when Hamlet's around. Hamlet's cute.

When Hamlet gets going on one of his long speeches we go *oh oh oh oh* like we are Hamlet's own girlfriend. Then this lady usher comes and tells us we have to be quiet. She's a total bitch.

*

A few days later.

The first week is now history at the Braidie Institute. Two weeks now without Adrienne.

This is me without my friends. I am nothing, zero, zip. A black mark on the horizon.

If I had to I could live on this beach for a long time—live on berries and fish and kelp. Trevor, remember how we'd plant ourselves up there in the bank? The perfect camouflage—we would spy on the blind just doing their every-day stuff: the little kids going ballistic, the old guys sucking back the lemonade. Remember them swimming? Bobbing around in their lifejackets, unaware that the sun is descending in some spectacular fashion. They had that way of turning their faces up to the sky—all weird and happy.

It floored me Trevor. I mean I'm sure their lives are usually even more dull and shitty and hideous than the rest of us but I used to imagine myself blind—how careful I would be. For my eighteenth birthday I would be given a dog. I would call him Henry. *There goes Henry and Braidie.* I never think about all the stuff I wouldn't be able to do, what I wouldn't be able to see. For once I am focusing on only the positive. The voice of mum would be proud of me.

BRAIDIE *goes back in time, she is twelve years old.*

We are blind: Adrienne, Amber, Jackie and me. We have made a huge pile of sand and leaves. We cover our eyes with a pair of old panty hose and leap off the bank. We turn each other around and around to see if we can point in the right direction—at the beach, the mountains, each other. We feel each other's faces, stomachs, breasts. *Definitely Braidie.* If it wasn't winter I would swim away, swim blind into the middle of the sea.

This is boring. Adrienne takes off her blind fold. We take off ours. We climb up the bank and hide in the laurel leaves. We think about going to the store to steal something: gum, matches, bath oil bubbles that squish in our pockets and leak all over our shirts. Sometimes Adrienne steals change and cans of beer from the people she baby-sits for. I confine my crimes to the General Store and believe I am a slightly less bad person.

Adrienne goes to light a smoke then stops. *Look* ... And we look out on the beach and there is Sofie. *What is It doing?* We haven't seen Sofie in ages. *God, look at* IT! Adrienne makes it sound as if Sofie is out there killing something. I squint in on her but Sofie is just hunched over a little book. Maybe Sofie still draws pictures of horses. Maybe she also likes trying to write poems and stories. The possibility that Sofie and I might have even one thing in common makes a little shift in me.

I'm going to get It. Adrienne is climbing down the vines. Sofie looks up and in the wrong direction: pure Sofie. And Adrienne is right there, grabbing Sofie by the ponytail.

What do you think you're doing?

Nothing. Sofie slams her book shut, she examines her feet.

What's in the book?

Nothing.

And Sofie tries to run, to bolt down the beach. Adrienne still has a hold of her hair, she pushes Sofie down. Sofie's head makes a little smack sound on the rock. It sounds phony— like a slap in the movies. And then her head is

45

bleeding and the blood looks phony too. And then we are all around Sofie. This is it. Adrienne is going to do something. And we are going to see. Then Adrienne is holding a covered elastic and a tangle of Sofie's hair.

Sofie is gone, running. And then everybody is running after her, someone is yelling *No No No* ... It isn't me.

Sofie mashes open her jeans falling on the barnacles. She starts climbing back up the blackberries and Adrienne is right there, grabbing on to her ankle.

I understand too now what Sofie wants to do. Sofie is going to ring the bell at the blind camp. You can hear that bell all over the island. But then Adrienne screams and we all stop breathing.

We watch Adrienne slide down the bank while Sofie scrambles away. We peer down at Adrienne on the sand, all curled up and quiet. *She's dead.* Amber announces.

BRAIDIE, *as a teenager again.*

But I knew Adrienne had just been stalled, shot, hit by a smooth black stone. And that you were there, you were with us Trevor, up in the maple tree. How much did you know all along? How much did you see? Adrienne came back from the dead a moment later. *Your brother is such an asshole.* Adrienne knew it was you but somehow it becomes Sofie's fault too. *Sofie and Trevor probably do it together, do it twenty times a day.*

We all lay there on the sand, joined at the head, spokes in a wheel. In my pocket, a pink plastic diary and a key. Of course it belonged to Sofie. I didn't show it to anyone. But I felt entitled, I found it, it was mine to keep and mine to see.

What was Sofie doing as we lay there on the beach? Were the others thinking about her too? How she might be stumbling in the back door of her house, trying to keep the blood and the dirt from getting over everything. *I fell, I slipped, I whacked my head on an alder tree.* We all understand that Sofie telling the truth isn't even a remote possibility.

BRAIDIE *goes back in time, she is twelve years old.*

Jackie shifts down, rests her head on my stomach. I place my head on Adrienne's. We make a chain. First Amber laughs then Jackie, all around the circle. I can feel the laughter and the skin of Adrienne's body, warm against my ear. And then, I'm laughing too and when we stop there's just our breath, rising and falling. I match my breath to Adrienne's perfectly.

*

The next day.

Mum comes thundering down the stairs last
night to announce she has given up. I point
out, as calmly as possible—*If you're going to give
up on someone you just give up. You don't tell
them about it.* Mum goes berserk. All this
screaming and crying and gnashing of teeth.
Then she notices the pictures, some of the
newspaper clippings tacked up around my
room. *I'm studying.*

And then she's screaming—*Cut the lip! Cut
all the nonsense about home schooling.* And she is
inside my room, mine, for the first time in a
year and a half. A complete violation of my
rights. *What is this stuff?* She is looking at this
cover from the Vancouver Province. *At least
SHE has a nice haircut.*

She's a killer—I tell her.

And mum takes me by the shoulders—*Look.*
She stares right into me, then her eyes fill up
and she touches my cheek. *Braidie?* It's worse
than anything, the voice of mum trying to be
my buddy, trying to be half-way sweet.

Get out. Her hands drop to her side. *This is
my room.* But she isn't moving. She gets me so
pissed off I just start flailing.

—*BRAIDIE use your words.*

—*All right. Fuck you mother.*

And she gets it, she finally gets it. She slams the door behind her. She's giving up on me.

I look at the girl, the picture of the girl who did it. The one in Victoria who held her head underwater until all was quiet. The one who held a smoke in one hand and held the girl under with the other, her foot on her back. She bragged about it. Maybe she made the telling of it into a joke because she doesn't know how else to try it out. *Did you hear the one about ...* Maybe she just snapped. I do that. I look at the picture again: she's a regular girl.

And she's hanging out on a Friday night in November, 1997— the moon is full, the air is clear. Usually the stars get lost in winter here. But on this night the stars are out, everyone is out, *under cover*, passing a joint, drinking vodka and sprite mixed in a can. Some are watching the sky and waiting because a Russian satellite is going to break through the earth's atmosphere tonight, right over Victoria. It will explode, light up all that black.

But this girl, this regular girl and one other girl are waiting for something else; they are waiting to teach someone a lesson. They've already phoned her up, they've called her out.

Because she is big, because she likes *that* boy. Because she is brown and she lost their book; because she doesn't fit and she lies. Because they can.

The girl they're going to get is miserable, that much is clear. Four different schools and two different foster homes in the past year. She keeps returning to family—her parents, her grandma and grandpa. And she keeps running away. And she doesn't know, doesn't get the plot, doesn't understand her part. So it starts.

The ones who watched, maybe they thought it wasn't real. Maybe as they yelled out or laughed they were actually frozen. Maybe they were so glad to not be that girl—whose hair is being held up to a lighter now—that they don't even know how to imagine shouting *stop*. Maybe they think that silence is the ticket, the only way to never end up like the girl.

Even the ones who didn't watch, who just heard about what happened, they carry the silence too—a dark present, passed hand to hand. When they get home maybe they will dream about being blind. Because they can't stand the replays anymore—how the girl looked up and begged for help.

Or maybe it's that boy in Burnaby last winter, how he wrote his goodbye note and climbed the rails on the Putallo Bridge.

Or maybe it's Sofie. Because just when you think it was all ancient history it starts again.

Trevor—remember how I went through the first five years of life hiding behind mum's bum whenever we were out in public? That's the trouble with staying silent. I can't move, even when I want to. And I start thinking Adrienne acts for me.

*

BRAIDIE *goes back in time, she is fourteen years old.*

It is dark now by 4:30. We miss the school bus on purpose so that we can hang out longer in town. *Mum—I'll be on the 6:30 ferry, pick me up* ... I'm doing what I do everyday after school, what I did practically every day in grade eight and in grade nine too. I am in the parking lot behind the school and I am waiting for Adrienne. High School is just like how movie stars describe making movies—there's a lot of waiting around.

It's raining hard; my hair is soaking wet—unbelievably ugly. There are about thirty of us hanging out. Some of the older guys have cars. These little pools of light—vibrating with music and bodies and smoke. And with Adrienne.

Right now she is in Justin Hannah's Dodge Caravan. She loves Justin and Justin, of course, treats her terribly. I think Justin is sort of an idiot. In fact I find a lot of Adrienne's guys are fairly gross.

Across from the parking lot every else lines up for the bus—shoving and smoking and fooling around. Except for one still shape, holding on to the bus sign like it's some sort of anchor. Sofie always has her hood up, rain or shine. From the back she looks like this giant version of ET. Sofie is something Adrienne seems to have forgotten. At lunch Sofie doesn't go to the cafeteria or behind the gym or the parking lot like the rest of us. She slinks along the edges of the halls; she walks away from the school. She walks around and around. She often eats lunch in a bus shelter, six blocks from our school. She doesn't hang out with other kids. She is certainly doing her very best to be invisible.

I have no idea why I feel I have to keep tabs on Sofie. I just do. Sometimes I follow her around. She has no idea; she has always been a fairly clued out individual. I go to the bus shelter after she's left to check it out. There are little rocks lined up along the sides and she's carved her initials—S.G.—into the seat. No doubt it all is charged with meaning in the weird world of Sofie. Maybe I'll give back her diary. I keep it at the back of my locker, just on the verge of handing it over. I never even finished reading the whole thing. It was too boring—just a regular girl. She doesn't let anyone in on anything.

I watch Sofie board the bus, always first on so that she can sit directly behind the driver. I watch the bus pull away just as Adrienne gets out of Justin's van.

Adrienne lights a cigarette and glares at me. Justin was supposed to give us a ride to the ferry but apparently now this is completely and totally out of the question. We walk—two and a half miles. I get home four hours late, the voice of mum waiting on the dock to tear a strip off of me.

*

A girl in the shape of a monster
A monster in the shape of a girl

It all starts again just three weeks ago, in the girls bathroom. Right after home room. I walk in. I'm not doing anything, I'm minding my own business, I just have to pee. Sofie is there. Applying this goofy blue eye-liner in a goofy blue line. Then guess-who comes kicking her way out of the end cubicle. Adrienne's been crying; her eyes are rabbity pink. No doubt there has been some new atrocity between her and Justin. *Let's go.* That's me, trying to head her off but Adrienne has already seen Sofie.

—*What are you looking at?* Sofie goes blank. She turns and fixes her sights on the tampax machine. *I asked you a question.* But Sofie is still in statue mode, uninhabited. No doubt Sofie's entire school life is an out of body experience.

Adrienne drops her Atlas on Sofie's foot. Sofie doesn't blink.

—*Pick it up.*

—*Let's go.*

—*I said pick it up.*

Do something, say something, anything, fight. Do something, say something, anything, fight...

But Sofie just bends over. And I hate her. As soon as she does it I know she's lost. Adrienne kicks Sofie down on all fours. All the work she'd put into being invisible, down the drain. Sofie is entirely visible—her legs are pink, her underwear covered in little blue circles.

Lovely. Sofie the horse. Sofie tries to get up and Adrienne's boot comes down in the centre of Sofie's back. *Did I say you could get up?* Sofie tries to turn her head around but Adrienne grabs her by the shirt. *Maybe the horse needs a drink of water.* Adrienne pulls Sofie over to the toilet.

And yes, finally. Sofie's head is turning, twisting away from Adrienne and ... turning toward me. *Braidie please.*

You do what you have to do.
You look down.
Like this.

And then you navigate your way to the door using only your peripheral vision.

When I walk down the hall, I feel all weird and pukey. I feel like everyone is staring at me. I don't go to English; I just walk around. And then I don't go to Math or P.E. At lunch I go looking for Sofie. I go to the bus shelter. S.G. still carved into the bench. Why wouldn't it be?

After school, when I get on the bus, Adrienne is waiting, waiting for me.

—*Adrienne. What happened?* But she doesn't know what I'm talking about, can't remember, just a regular day. *What happened to Sofie?*

—*Nothing happened.* I see the empty seat behind the driver on the bus, Sofie's seat. A tremor starts, way down low on the floor of the ocean. *With someone like Sofie you never have to actually DO anything.* My hands are shaking, the bus pulls out. *Shut up* says Adrienne. *Stop breathing like a pervert.*

But Adrienne seems miles away now, deflated, her face behind her hair all white and skinny.

And she's gone. The friend I loved is gone. All that's left is the shape of a girl.

FOR EMERGENCY ONLY. I push out the window and it fans out from the bottom unnaturally. I puke all down the side of the bus. The driver lets me off. I walk back to school. I go right into the girls' bathroom. I wash my face. When I turn off the tap I hear a sound, from the last cubicle.

Sofie is sitting on the lid of the toilet. Her lips all puffed up and purple. When she sees who it is, she covers her head. *Don't worry ...* She's acting like I'm going to hit her, which is so crazy. *I never did anything.* I bet she wishes you were there Trevor, hiding out behind the tampax machine, waiting to get off a good shot at me.

Sofie rocks back and forth then all of a sudden she smashes her head into the side of the stall.

We did a good job. Even Sofie hates Sofie.

*

A bell sounds as in the beginning.

Sound carries across water. On that full moon
night, in Victoria, the word goes out that a girl
was killed, that girl. Maybe there are groups of
kids in schoolyards, malls ... *Really?* And by the
time her body is found—hundreds of kids
know and hundreds of kids don't tell. Who is
the one who told the unthinkable to their mum
or their teacher? Who marched into the police
station and said *see here, enough is enough?* I'll
bet you a million dollars everyone thinks it
wasn't a girl.

*

I always thought it was the voice of mum that
made you escape Trevor. But I'm wondering
now if you moved to Whistler to get away from
me. In fact you might be ecstatic to know I am
well on my way to becoming the official island
outcast. I just wanted you to know one thing.
One tiny thing that'll probably be the end of
me.

Mum is forcing me to abandon homeschooling. I agreed, on the condition, that the
voice of mum no longer speak to me. So yesterday the now defunct Braidie Institute went on
our first and last field trip—to the Island

Community Preschool. Remember preschool?
Remember what a big deal it was?

They have this snazzy new building now. I'm
hanging out at the fence like some kind of
psycho. Watching all these kids smash into
each other on their trikes and kicking around
in the mud puddles. All these nutty four-year-
olds doing their usual things. And Annie
comes out. Her hair is all gray now. But she is
still the same because this boy is hanging off
her arm by his teeth and she doesn't even
notice. You can tell she still thinks all kids are
just dandy.

Then Annie spots me. *Braidie!* You'd think I
was God or something. You'd think I was the
greatest thing she's ever seen. And Annie
comes running over. She smells like play
dough. She opens the gate for me.

A spot shines brightly in front of BRAIDIE, *she
steps into the light.*

And I understand for the first time what I
have to say and how long I've been practicing.

I wish to report the behaviour of ...
I fear for ...
I'm scared. Scared for the safety of another girl.
That she might do something crazy. Her name is
Sofie. She has been treated in a despicable way by
many people ... including me.

Annie doesn't say anything. For the longest time she just nods. And then when she finally does speak it's in this weird whisper because she probably hates me. She will go with me to my school, to the principal. I tell her—*okay*.

She holds me tightly. Maybe she thinks I'm going to escape. Her arms still fit around me.

*

A bell sounds again then BRAIDIE *looks up.*

Sound carries across water. The girl in Victoria is discovered after eight days, her body seen floating from the air above. The stories were endless, the stories about how it all happened. Most of them weren't true. The only real story is the one told by her body, silently. This bruising beneath her eyes, the black nose and cheeks. The broken arm and the star burnt into her forehead.

A bell sounds fourteen times.

Sometimes I dream she got away, swam straight out into the ocean, maybe floated off on a log boom. Where? Not south to the States, not here. I don't know how to imagine it; I don't know where her safe place might be. I only know how to go backwards.

Braidie goes back in time, she is eight years old.

We are eight years old. We are all planting our toes in the edge of the water. We're at the blind beach, it's summer, the water is foamy and brown around our feet. We are all wearing life jackets. Adrienne, Amber, Sofie and me. The jackets make us feel like we can go anywhere, do anything—deep water, waves, you name it, all these possibilities.

We are brave, we are perfect—girls.

The End

Jewel

The original version of *Jewel* was performed at The Banff Centre, February, 1985. This version, revised and expanded substantially, premiered at Tarragon Theatre in Toronto, April, 1987 with the following cast:

MARJORIE   Joan MacLeod

Director: Andy McKim
Set & Costume Designer: Linda Muir
Lighting Designer: Heather Sherman
Stage Manager: Beth Bruck

The play is set in the Peace River Valley on Valentine's Day, 1985, in Marjorie's mobile home. MARJORIE CLIFFORD is 30 years old.

The play runs approximately one hour with no intermission.

Prologue

MARJORIE is standing in her nightgown beside a full bucket of fresh milk. She speaks directly to the audience.

MARJORIE

Valentine's through the ages. You are six years old and folding up this gigantic piece of white tissue paper until it's the size of your hand. Then attacking it with these dull little scissors, chopping the corners off, driving a hole right through the middle. But when you unfold it— pure magic: triangles and diamonds pinwheeling out from the centre, a thousand crescent moons. So you cut out this heart and paste it onto red cardboard. Print his name very carefully, then your own name, right along side. It's so special you can barely stand it. Only when you get to school you discover that every girl in your class has done the very same thing. And the most popular boy in the world just stuffs all those valentines into his desk without saying a word. By the end of the afternoon you realize that some of those hearts have turned into paper airplanes, some into spitballs. Valentine's through the ages. Alright.

You are thirteen and at the Claresholme Teen Stomp and everything is dumb: the red punch, the heart-shaped plates, Claresholme, the records that are all old and country. But the dumbest thing ever is Lucy who you're down here visiting.

Lucy is fifteen and what your mother calls mature—meaning she has big tits, smokes and is also stupid. She visited you last month and was afraid to get on an escalator. But it gets worse. Because right now, Lucy is dancing with some wonderful boy and she's danced ten thousand times since she got here. You haven't been asked once. You also don't care a damn but there goes Lucy again, right up to the boys lining the rear wall of the gym. She tells them to go dance with her cousin Marjorie. That's you. And it's like all your nerves have gone electric and the air too. Nobody moves. They're just lined up like some kind of firing squad, a big string of monkeys and now all you can look at is their boots and the dumb floor. Lucy says please and that you're an orphan, which isn't true, but you still just die. No matter how many times you tell dumb-ass Lucy she still wants to hear about orphanages and that.

Then you notice it—black cowboy boots two feet in front of you. And someone you're afraid to look at is asking you to dance. Okay. It's a slow song. You decide to kill yourself but there you are now. You can do it. Damp hands bumping together. His neck is red as a brick. He speaks. "Where you from?" And you're still afraid to look at him but by some miracle you manage it, "Calgary."

Then two perfect minutes, moving ever-so-small, one side to another. You just want to take a peek. His eyes are flat and brown as a frozen puddle and staring straight at your cousin Lucy. Suddenly he looks clean into you and tells you he wouldn't live in Calgary if it was the last place on earth. And it feels so stupid and mean, "That's fine," you tell him. That's just great. Then you explain how the Beatles love Calgary and that they're moving there next month.

Everything changes. He is looking at you special. Some of the others are too. Questions come from everywhere. "When? What would they do that for? Have you met them?" And for the first time, you, are right at the centre of a very perfect world. Invented, but still perfect. Valentine's through the ages. You are thirteen years old and dizzy with love.

Two years later, you're at a sleepover. Nine other girls there in flannel nighties. You've all arrived with an inch of liquor, stolen from your folks' rye and scotch and gin bottles.

You mix this up with a twenty-sixer of Tahiti Treat and sit cross-legged in a circle, passing the bottle around. Every time you take a sip, you tell a truth—how you went to second with so and so. Who it is you're really in love with this week. It's all marvelous. It's all made up. You're half-sick with pink liquor and trying to French inhale Peter Jackson cigarettes. You light a candle and listen to Joni Mitchell sing *Both Sides Now* eleven times in a row. You're delirious with sadness. You phone up a dozen boys, say something absolutely filthy then hang up the phone. This liquor in your gut. This tingling in your legs, You are fifteen years old and sick with love.

Valentine's through the ages marches on. You've been going to the university and are all grown up. You have a boyfriend—this range management student who comes from the Arctic Circle. Well nearly. Range management: the choreography *(beat)* of cows. You met in February but now it's August. You're camping near his folks' place in northern Alberta. You're out of your territory. And you love it. Because there is something about him and this place that's like coming home after a long, long journey. And it's true in a way, coming home.

The inside of your blue nylon tent sweats in the morning sun. Through this gauzy half-moon of a window mosquitoes crash around; two little kids collect beer bottles in a potato sack, eat O'Henry bars at six a.m.

The cattle arranger, with his sleeping bag zipped up with yours, is enjoying the sleep of the dead. You are enjoying this chance to examine his face: high cheekbones, lashes like a woman's, black hair sticking out in a million directions. Out of your territory. And last night, at six minutes to midnight, he asked you to stay out of your territory forever. Marriage. "Marry me, Marjorie." There's this land he's wanting to buy and no money for cattle yet but the oil patch is right around the corner. He's got his welder's papers. The money will flow. Maybe five winters of working out then full-time farming or ranching or whatever. He talks about buying a milk cow and *(picking up bucket)* you nearly pass out with the romance of it. One of his hands is against his heart as if he were taking a pledge. And the other one is meandering up your nightgown. Valentine's through the ages.

A country song starts up softly on radio.

Six years later now. You're still crazy with love.

Scene One

MARJORIE is now in her trailer. She turns up the radio and carries her bucket into the kitchen area. While singing along to the radio she pours milk into two large glass jars and places them in the fridge. She removes another milk jar from the fridge and skims the cream off the top. She listens to Message Time. She drinks beer.

MARJORIE

Christ I'm thirsty. Thirsty for everything except milk. Your dad made this beer. I mean it doesn't taste terrible but it sort of leaves fur on your teeth. No one can really make good beer, they all just think they can and are dying for you to drink this flat stuff that's clear as mud. Oh well, Harry. You know what they say to do with failed beer? Drink it.

RADIO

And that's it for Country Countdown tonight. Happy Valentine's. And you better snuggle up

to the one you love because, according to
Environment Canada, it's a chilly thirty-three
below in Fort St. John tonight and it looks like
it's going to dip down even lower.

MARJORIE

You hear that Harry? Cozy up.

RADIO

And now Message Time. The link between you
and your loved ones. A community service
brought to you by CKNL North Country.

MARJORIE

You'll have to stay quiet for a minute. Think
you can manage that?

RADIO

To Connie Brown: Happy Valentine's. Wish I
could be there with love from Stanley. To
Cynthia, Ruthie and Jason: home on Saturday,
love from your daddy, Jason Senior. To Beatrice
George: call Credit Union immediately, very
important.

MARJORIE

Poor Beatrice. They're broke.

RADIO

To Billy Gustafson: your cattle are out and in
Chevron property south of Fish Creek. Remove
at once. To Marjorie Clifford:

MARJORIE
Yes sir.

RADIO
Your order is in at Buckerfields'. Will be delivered on the seventeenth.

MARJORIE
Well it's about time.

RADIO
To Rebecca Cochrane: not coming home as planned, will call on Saturday, Aubrey Cochrane. To Sally Harper: Happy Valentines. You are my one and only, love Frank.

MARJORIE *turns off radio.*

MARJORIE
You know Harry? I was listening to Message Time. When was it? Christmas Eve, years ago. You were working for Esso out on Cotcho Lake. I'd just come up from school and missed you by half a day. I mean that first year of being married we must've spent all of ten minutes together. So me and Deb are drinking eggnog and listening to the messages. They're gushy as hell. "To Ruth in Dawson who I met in the bar last night. I love you more than life itself." That sort of thing. Even Debbie got something half-way romantic from Walter. And I'm sitting there waiting then getting worried that maybe you forgot. Then realizing you'd never do that and getting very excited and it comes. "To

73

Marjorie Clifford. Merry Christmas. The calf will be needing her worm shot on the twenty-seventh." Period.

Was I pissed off Harry? I threw my eggnog at the radio. And then I start to stand up for you. Defend your good name. Telling Debbie how you're really very romantic but in a private sort of way. Which was true enough I suppose.

A dog barks in the distance.

But Jesus. Worm shot.

No! You've been outside for all of two seconds. Go chase a weasel. That dog, Harry. Remember going down to Beaverlodge to buy him? Staying in that very lousy motel called Shady Glenn or Palm Grove—some Prairie name like that. And the guy with the litter's explaining that this dog's part wolf. I mean there's no person north of Edmonton that doesn't own a dog part wolf. It can be purebred Chihuahua and people round here would still say "Careful. That dog's got wolf in it." So we buy this thing that looks like a guinea pig and, in a fit of inspiration, we name him *(beat)* Wolf.

And on the way home, he's sitting on the floor of the truck, quivering for a hundred miles. He hasn't changed. I mean he's big now. In fact he's fat. His only goal in life seems to be figuring out a way of never going outside. I think Wolf would rather live with my folks in the city, eat canned dog food, and lie around all day on their wall-to-wall.

I meant to explain why I never came home last night. No Harry. I was not out fooling around. I was at Debbie's. She put the kids to bed and we made this massive supper. Walter had just gone back to the bush and I guess the guy that picked him up had this bag of shrimp, fresh from the coast that morning.

So we shucked them or whatever the hell it is you do with shrimp. And we made this white wine sauce. Then drank what was left over which was about a gallon each. Deb's doing fine. I mean her and Walter are in debt over this new tractor like you wouldn't believe but they're making out. Where was I? Deb's last night—right.

So we're just sitting there talking and getting very drunk and there's this knock at the door. It's not even eight-thirty but feels around midnight and I'm thinking, shit—it's your dad. Then it dawns on me that Munroe's never knocked on a door in his life. He just comes in and yells, "I'm here! Where's the coffee?"

Well. Guess who? Guess who wears sensible shoes and overcoats and, more than likely, have a good case of pimples on the go? It's the Mormons.

Come all the way from the state of Utah to bring us the word of God. I don't get up off the couch. That is to say I'm incapable of getting off the couch. And I'm thinking—this is great. We actually live in a place that needs missionaries. I mean I know they do their business in the cities too but I'm pretending the North is like darkest Africa and that Deb and me have rings through our noses and these big, black breasts hanging out front, like torpedoes, like National Geographic. And the younger one, he's all of eighteen or something. He asks me if I've been saved and I tell him, "UNGOWA!"

These two are very embarrassed. They pack up their stuff, give us some pamphlets, head out into forty below in this little Japanese car. We laugh about it for a while longer then end up feeling bad. I mean it's like being drafted, it's something they have to do.

I stayed overnight. Which is something I do quite often when Walter's off in the bush. We sleep in the same bed and hug and that but it's not gay or anything. It's just very nice when you're on your own to have other people close by. And we understand one another quite well. Debbie and me.

A dog barks in the distance.

No! Go make some friends. That dog. Wolf
must've had something very horrible happen to
him when he was real young. Old Wolf and
me, eh? Or maybe before we got hold of him
that guy beat him, or his mother tried to eat
him. Yeah, that suits Wolf. He's just hanging
around with all his brothers and sisters, trying
to have a good time and his mother tries to eat
him.

Remember when we tried to take him
hunting for lynx? Wolf is obsessed with
thoughts of his own death and refuses to leave
the truck. Your wife, who is me, is also
obsessed with death but is equally obsessed
with making this marriage work. Lucky for you,
the shits for me. How's your beer there, Harry?
You're looking a little pale around the edges
tonight.

Wanna dance? C'mon dance with me.

Marjorie *turns on radio and dances to a fiddle
waltz.*

It's Valentine's night at the Ranch Cabaret.
We're dancing to a band called Hot Lightning.
Dancing tight and slow. Your shirt smelling
like cedar and diesel. Smoke. We've been ice
fishing all day. The sky just getting heavy with
snow when we leave for town, the dark coming

in. By the time we get there, these big flakes.
Everything pretty as Christmas cards.

Your folks are there. Your mother waltzing
bolt upright and scared, shy at being in town.

Your eyes in her face—that wonderful jade.
Munroe leading her, proud and near drunk.
His arm around me at the table for the first
time. Telling how when you were little you
stole his truck and sunk it in the lake. All of us
proud and near drunk. This mirror ball's
sprinkling light all round the room and across
your face. We've just gone into life-time debt
for buying the land and this trailer. I believe we
are perfectly happy. That is to say, I, am
perfectly happy.

RADIO

And that's our request waltz for this evening
and goes out to Mr. and Mrs. R. Johnson. And
now more easy listening on CKNL, your north
country station.

MARJORIE turns off the radio.

MARJORIE

And on the way home in the pick-up, all four of
us squeezed inside, your dad says—"Look at
them cheeks of Marjorie's, all glowy and red. I
like that in a woman. Looks freshly slapped."
And I think, great, I've married into a family of
insane people. But I figured it out pretty

quick—this father and son. When you went
down, Munroe was the only one that didn't
mind my staying quiet, that could keep
comfortable with it.

They're still looking out for me, Harry.
They're both doing fine. *(pause)* That was nice.
You are some dancer. In fact you're wearing me
out.

Today I was at the Co-op in town, buying
groceries and that. This kid is pushing the
buggy. I think he's one of Beatrice's boys but
then it's hard to keep track. And this other kid
who's working there yells from across the
parking lot, "Hey Mitchell! What's got four
legs, is three hundred feet tall and goes down
on Newfoundland?" And this kid Mitchell looks
real embarrassed. You can just tell he's praying
his buddy over there will shut up. Because old
Mitchell knows who I am. I mean I am one
hell of a famous widow Harry. We're talking
Time magazine. Reporters all the way from
Texas braving forty below and gravel roads just
to get a picture of me and Wolf. And this kid
yells it again, "Mitch? What's a thousand feet
tall, has four legs and goes down on
Newfoundland?" And I end up apologizing!
Saying I've always been one to make jokes
about anything and everything. This idiot, he
yells it out *(beat)* "The *Ocean Ranger!*" *(beat)*
Old Mitch practically has a heart attack right on

the spot. By the time he's got the truck loaded it looks like he's decided to be a priest.

You know I always thought it was a ridiculous name—the *Ocean Ranger*. Like a speedboat full of Girl Guides. And when you first got the job I just panicked because I didn't know how to imagine you there. That's important Harry. It's important to women who have husbands who work out to know how to imagine them in a place. I mean all I had to do was drive into town or walk to your dad's to see a rig on the ground, to set you somewhere. And usually you were just up around Nelson and I knew that if I really went squirrelly I could jump in the truck and find you. But Newfoundland! That is practically four thousand miles away. Right from the start it felt wrong. I mean we're supposed to be farmers and there you are out on this floating thing in the middle of some ocean. The Atlantic Ocean.

And when I got the call that you'd gone down, all I could think was that you were drifting, that you might sink for a minute, then get caught up in kelp or some current, and set off again, that you'd never settle. You'd never arrive on something solid again. And I thought about that Harry, non-stop. Thought about that for fourteen months without a break.

Then I'm living with my folks, and my mother, she signs me up for some god-awful thing called a grieving workshop. All this group stuff going on that just makes me mental. I mean this is a very private business if you ask me. Everyone wanting me to come to terms with this. Those sort of expressions are another thing that makes me crazy. They're just pieces of air. And all I'm really wanting is for everyone just to leave me alone. Some church ran this thing and they're tossing scripture around like a volleyball. I mean as if that's going to fill my bed or help me make payments.

Okay, we got our money since then. But I mean this isn't some cheque that just showed up in the mail one day. This is after two years of drawn out bullshit with lawyers and Louisiana accents. Every time you open the paper or a magazine or letter, more stuff about the *Ocean Ranger*. What I want, through the whole inquiry, is to narrow it down to one man. But we couldn't even narrow it down to one company. But it's still what I keep wanting, just pare it all down. Leave me one man, up there on the top floor, behind some marble top desk.

I want him to say "Yup, I'm your boy, it was my fault. My fault about the design flaws, the lack of survival suits, my fault about the evacuation procedure and that the lifeboats would've gone down in a lake. I'm your boy. Not that I meant any of it but I sure as hell did screw things up. You think safety is top priority but it gets lost somewhere along the way. You get tested like that and completely fail the test. I screwed up. Big time."

I don't want to cause this man any harm. But I would like to place him aboard a drilling platform, after midnight in February, over a hundred miles from the coast of Newfoundland. An alarm calls this man from sleep and onto a deck that is pitch black and tipped over fifteen degrees and all covered in ice. The wind is screaming. Salt water and snow pelt his face. Everybody is running around and nobody knows what to do. He is in his pajamas and being lowered in a life raft with twenty other men, into a sea of fifty foot waves.

Then I would reach down and lift that man up from this terrible place just like the hand of God come to save him. Remove him from all that terror and certain death. I'd place him somewhere warm and dry. Relief here and family. Take his shivering hand inside my own and turn his hand over and over and over. Until he sees it. Palm up and attached and staring straight at him. His hand is the hand of God and he could have gathered them all up. Saved eighty-four men from the North Atlantic. He chose not to.

And I don't care who owns you mister. I don't
care if you're ODECO or Mobil Oil, a fed or
provincial. My sadness,—my husband's
death—it was handmade by someone.

You know at first, right after, I thought my
insides were made out of paper. Very white
paper. I would even walk carefully because I
thought something might rip inside. Where am
I? Right. We were talking about the grieving
workshop. I go off in a corner with a Bible just
so they won't bug me. And I actually found
something that made sense: the book of
Genesis, page one, "Let the waters teem with
living creatures and let the birds fly above the
earth within the vault of Heaven. And so it was,
God created great whales."

Well. I hold onto those lines like a goddamn
life jacket. I start pretending you are this very
fine whale with the sun on your back and just
having the life of Riley in general.

You see, Harry. What I loved about that is I'm
thinking you have no heart and no memory. I
mean I know that whales have warm blood and
a heart and that but it's not the sort that makes
you barge through everything like some open
nerve. And I thought, that's the ticket. No heart
and no memory. I thought that was about the
best way to live that anyone had ever come up
with.

Very crazy stuff. Well old friend. (MARJORIE
looks at her ring) You don't have a heart and you
don't have a memory anymore. I suppose that
part's the truth. But I do. Even this summer.
I'd just moved back here and everyone was so
worried that I'd go crazy again. And sure
enough, that's when I started having these little
night-time chats of ours. But it wasn't like now.

I'd tell you about the kid driving grain truck,
the one helping out with harvest. I'd bring him
out these sandwiches at noon. Because of the
heat, he would take off his shirt and this line of
sweat would sort of weep down his belly. We
lean against the wheel of the truck for shade
and drink ice water out of a thermos, passing it
back and forth.

And I told you I took him to the granary. The
air is very cool in there. We take off all our
clothes without looking at one another. He
folds up his jeans and makes a pillow, like for
under my head. The floor boards and loose
seed cut into the backs of my legs. Everything
smells very clean and very dry. Like gravel. And
I mean this kid is really inside. And he's
moving above me and on me and all around
me. And it's like there are these thousands of
minnows that have just been sleeping under
my skin forever and all at once they rush for
the surface. And it's ... it's, (beat) bravery. And
I think, fuck you, Harry! Dying and leaving me

is about the most gutless thing anyone could ever do.

All those stories about that kid driving grain truck? I made everyone of them up. Just wanting to make you jealous. Just trying to make you mad. Trying every trick in the book to get some kind of response. I mean he was barely seventeen or something That's called the Angry Phase, Harry. I think I'm starting to come out of it though.

I'll tell you a story that's true. There is a guy teaching school here that I've gone out with a few times. Some dinners in town. Last week we went to a play in Dawson Creek. He's a very nice man. Sort of shy. Or maybe it's lack of character. No. There's something quite good there.

He comes from Vancouver which is kind of an excuse but you know what he reminds me of? Me. When I first got here. All set to live on roots and berries, grow our own vegetables and animals and furniture. Seeing your folks' place for the first time I remember thinking—this is great—big old log house, smoke in the chimney. Your mum's real warm to me and she's making bread or canning moose or something equally terrific. But Munroe. It's afternoon and he's watching television. He doesn't even look up when we're introduced. Rude old bugger, I think but hating it just as much that he's watching TV instead of trimming wicks or milking some creature. We leave and on the way to the truck I can hear him yelling at his grandson, "Don't lick that cat. You'll get leukemia."

His name is Gordon, Harry. This school teacher guy ... Gord. I don't like his name one bit. Monday night I was over at his place for the first time. It's all cleaned up which it probably is anyway but I still like it, this making me feel special. He's cooked jackfish, wrapped up in some kind of leaves. Baked apples.

His place is all cedar and just half-done because he bought from Wilson who went bankrupt like you said he would. Gordon is determined with me. Serious as a machine.

The smell of wood makes me crazy. First winter with you in that cabin? Because we're just married I don't care a damn at first that we've built this little box to live in with wood that's green as lettuce. And that you stick to the wall every time you touch it. That there's no power or water and nearly no windows. That making coffee means half a day's work. But then I begin to notice everything; nothing is smooth, it's dark all the time, my clothes are alive with sawdust and the walls are alive with sap. So it starts. Small at first but eventually this enormous longing, desperate and ashamed. I want to live in a trailer. I need to live in a mobile home.

Gordon asked me to stay overnight. But I didn't. Or maybe I'm telling you lies again. Maybe I got him drunk on rye and coke; sex crazed widow flattens newcomer. You know I don't think I ever lied to you once the whole time we were together. But now, Jesus. I did this when I was little too, make up stuff to put in my diary.

But this, Harry, is the goods on Gordon. This is a story that's true. I didn't stay overnight but I did go to bed with him. I'm just telling you, not asking permission. It was alright. The best part being those very pure times when thinking stops. Just touch, react. But the flipside is thinking at a million miles an hour. How it is still your body that I know better than my own. How being held by living arms, hands, brings home what a body must be like lifeless. All the women wanted the bodies found, all the families of the victims. I never thought it'd be like that. You'd think lost would be better than dead. A strand of hope, invisible thin. But it makes you crazy, never knowing a hundred percent. It was way harder in the long run.

I am glad of meeting Gordon. Gord. I'm not saying you two would've hit it off in a huge way but I do like him, Harry. It's quite wonderful to have that small leap in the gut again when I know he's coming over, that kind of thing.

Wolf thinks of him as a minor God. Just lies at his feet with his paws up in the air like he's waiting to be sacrificed or trying to communicate telepathically that's he's trapped in a trailer with a maniac.

Wolf and me went for a walk on Sunday down to the lake. You know what he's doing? Sniffing around and making circles. Peeing on everything in sight and acting like a general lunatic. I'm explaining to him that it's February for God's sake and all the bears are asleep and to quit being so damn antsy. Then it dawns on me—he's still looking for your scent. I mean it's been three years but Wolf's still after your scent. And of course everything is froze solid and you can't smell a thing but whatever. Wolf is thinking you're around every corner, maybe skidding out birch for the woodpile or ice fishing or I don't know what dogs think.

So we get to the shore and there's these three kids from the reserve skating out on the lake. Boys, maybe seven years old. Needless to say, Wolf is scared of them. He stands on the shore rocking back and forth, quivering like a race horse. These kids are banging around a soccer ball with these big plastic baseball bats. Wolf is dying to get out there. He wants to run and bark and fool around with those kids and just

be a regular dog. But he can't do it. He just
stays there and yelps, does a few circles around
me. And for once I don't give him shit. I just
pat his head and let him be. Poor old Wolf. Just
wanting to be a regular dog. Everyone else
wanting him to be that way too. But Wolf's got
a few things figured out. He knows his limits.
Feels real good about those pats on the head.

So we just sat there for a long time, watching
those kids skate and the sun going down. I love
that time of day in winter. Used to be I hated
the night coming but it's alright now. I mean
it's not out-and-out terror anymore. Not all the
time at least.

Just a few more things, Harry. Then I'm
going to bed. They finally got me going to
another widows' group at the Elks twice a
month. In Newfoundland, they've got a group
just for *Ranger* families and it's supposed to be
great. But this bunch, I don't know. There's a
couple of new ones there who are in a very bad
way and it is good to talk things out with them
... support your sisters, that kind of stuff. But
there's this one woman there, she's from town,
works at the Bay, around your mum's age. And
she says that widowhood, it's like checking into
a motel for one night. One night that lasts the
rest of your life. I mean let's face it. The Elks is
about the most depressing way to spend an
evening that's ever been invented.

Then this lady says that nothing feels like home anymore. It's like we're all just waiting to get to another place. And I thought—right, Not that I think I'm going to another place. It's just that it feels like that ... the waiting.

You know how when you stay in a motel everything looks different—the bed, the pattern on the carpet? Even some dumb old TV show that you've watched every night of your life seems nearly exotic when you're in a motel. Very new.

Or those summers in Calgary before I met you. I had this really terrible job in an insurance office. Really punching the clock. Working in this little room without any windows. But every Friday at ten o'clock I'd have to go to the Treasury Branch. And I'd step out onto Centre Street and the world looked different: the bus stop right out front, even the way people walked. Everything transformed and clear and spooky, all at the same time.

So maybe that lady had a point, but she hasn't figured out the whole thing completely. I mean the world certainly does feel like a motel just in that everything looks so different. But you know Harry? Part of me likes that. It makes a walk with Wolf or just making dinner nearly miraculous.

I know. When we went to visit my folks and on the way down we stayed in Edmonton in that rather swanky place. We fooled around, practically overdosed on Cable TV. And we got room service for breakfast, opened the curtains up really wide and there's this apartment across the way. We watched all these people run around and get ready for work. The window's acting like a magnifying glass, everyone looks bigger than life. Even the air is defined and lively, just sparkling with light.

Okay. Sometimes I do feel like I'm just visiting here or stuck on the shore like old Wolf, not really able to get involved in anything. And very, very scared of going out on the ice again.

But I'll tell you something. I am beginning to feel again and part of me just loves staying in a motel. So maybe it's because I'm so much younger than most of them at the Elks but I'm not just waiting, not anymore. Not held down by that sadness. I mean I know it's part of me but it can't run the show forever. *(MARJORIE looks at her ring)* What do you think of that? My perfect jewel.

And what that lady from the Bay doesn't know or anybody else is that you got through to me. Valentine's through the ages. 1982.

You are about to slam, face first, into such a storm. But not yet. Maybe it's still quiet out there, just for a moment. I hope so. Wolf and me have been down at the barn, checking on things. I mean the animals would have to be doing something absolutely bizarre for us to see anything wrong but whatever. It's just before noon. I come in the kitchen, the radio's on. And there it is. First one out of the gate, a Valentine's message, short and sweet and probably sent the day before but meant to be mine now. I carry it around inside, hold onto it all day. It sends me to bed warm. Loud and clear. You love me. You got through.

Then late that night another message, hand delivered by an embarrassed RCMP. The rig has been evacuated. The constable offers to wait with me. They will call again in an hour on his car radio. I apologize for not having a phone, for all his trouble. I make tea. Wolf has gone wild. He can't believe his good luck. All this activity in the middle of the night.

Evacuated. What does it mean? Bombed out villages, buildings. Living in an air raid shelter. Living. He has left the rig and is in a lifeboat. There is a bad storm, a fifty foot sea.

How high? Like a grain elevator, fir tree. No. Too tall. I know. Me and Lucy are at Uncle Ray's, spitting down from the loft to where the cowshit is, "You kids get the hell down from there. You want to fall fifty feet and land on your heads?" That's when I know. Anything that big and made out of water is a deadly thing. But don't think it or it will be true and my fault. My legs are weak as bread. I grab hold of the counter and the kitchen floor moves like a raft underneath me. And there you are, clear as ice for a single moment. In a little boat, wearing that awful parka from Sears.

The horn on the police car blasts out of nowhere. Twice. Wolf and the police go to get the message on the radio phone. And I know it again but don't believe it for a second. Not on your life. I should go to Munroe's because your mother believes in God and I don't. I didn't mean it. The RCMP catches me down on my knees on the cold linoleum. He shakes his head. This is very hard for him, trying to tell me that my husband is dead.

But he doesn't tell me that. He says the rig has gone down and two of the lifeboats but the third boat is still out there. That means you. I know it.

But then this cop tells me they said not to have much hope. And I slap him across the back of the head.

I should've listened to him. It would've made the next few days a lot easier. All that waiting and glued to the radio. I should go to

Newfoundland but I'm afraid of flying now, of moving, of leaving the ground. Then the names of the dead are just read over the radio, in Munroe's kitchen. Confirmed. At the service, someone from your company is there telling me how sad this has made him. What I don't realize at the time is he can't apologize because it might make them liable. If you'd worked for Mobil itself, they wouldn't even have tried to make contact after the accident. Just hear it on the news with everyone else.

It doesn't start for a week or so because I suppose I'm in shock but I relive your death for a long, long time. You're in the lifeboat that nearly made it. That's what all the widows think. We think alike. I can't go through that stuff anymore.

Nearly midnight, Harry. Valentine's through the ages is coming to a close. Remember how I told you that first message sent me to bed warm? It's still there. A little bit.

MARJORIE *removes her ring.*

But wearing this forever. I don't know. I don't think it's such a great idea anymore. Does that make sense? I hope so. It does for me and I guess that's the important part.

It always felt so mean that it had to be Valentine's Day, that it was the last day you were alive. But I'm not so sure anymore.

This is what I'm sure of. You loved me. You got through.

The End